Chase in New York

Written by Simon Cheshire
Illustrated by Sarah Horne

Ed and Lin were with their dad. He went to lots of places to take photos.
New York Times

This time they were all going to New York.

“Look at all those yellow taxis!” said Ed.
“And all those tall buildings!” said Lin.

“Yes, they are called skyscrapers,” said Ed. “There are hundreds of skyscrapers in New York!”

"There is so much to see," said Ed. "Where to first?"

"Let's go to that park," said Lin.

Just then, there was a shout.

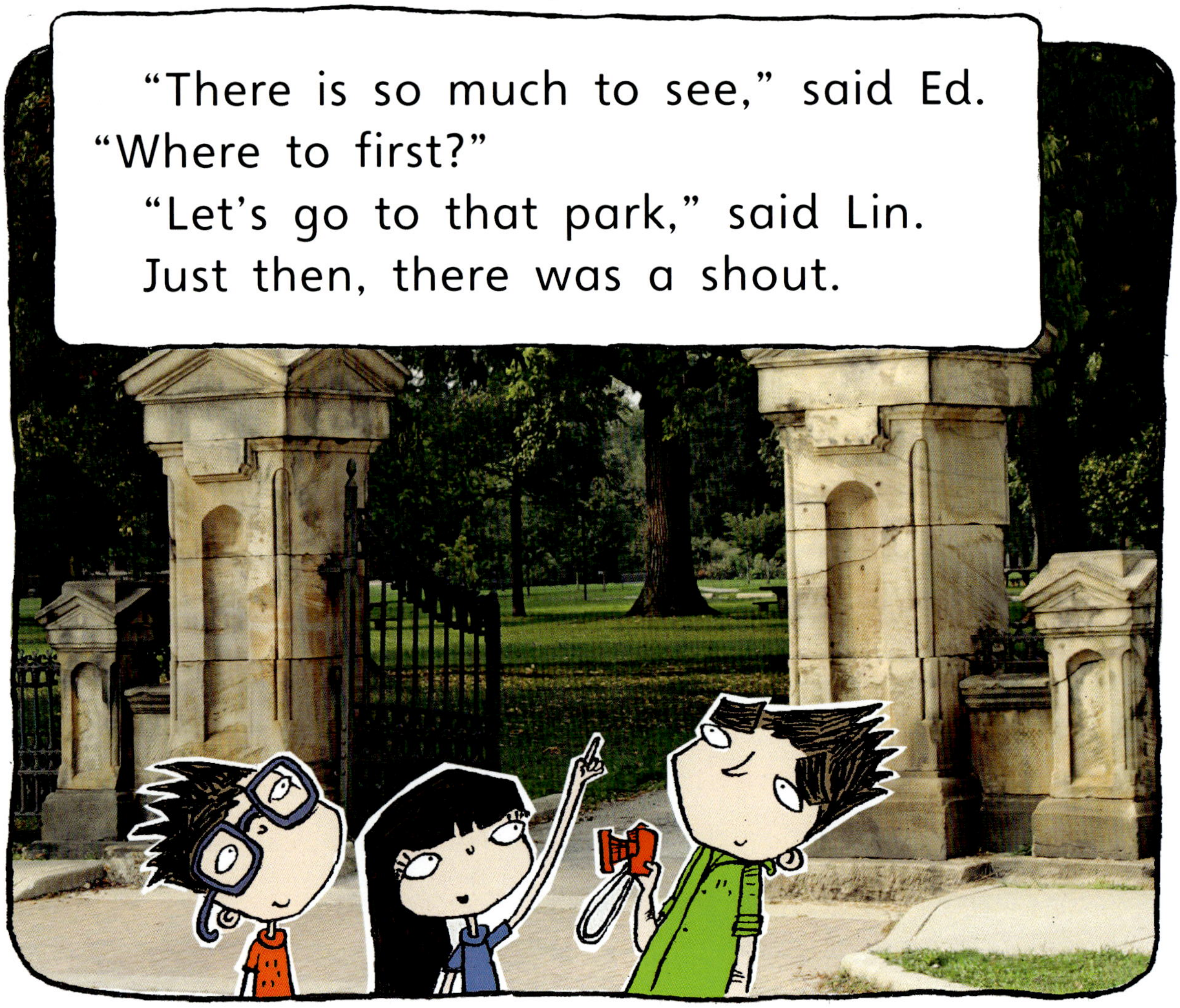

"HELP! My bag has been stolen!"

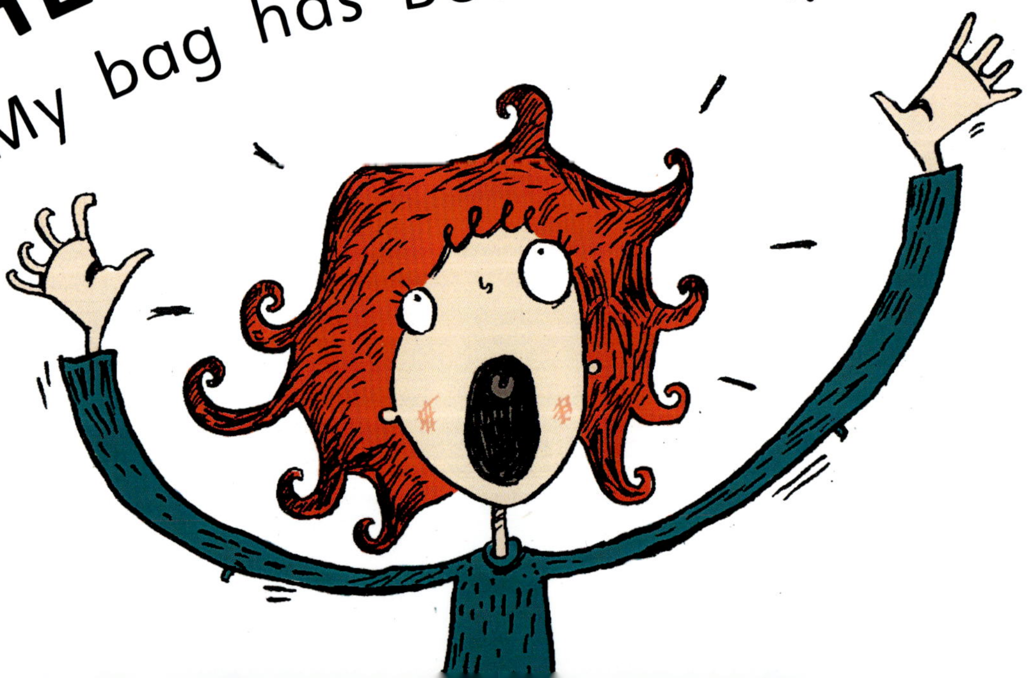

A man ran past them.
He had a mask on his face
and he was carrying a bag.

"That man has stolen the lady's bag!"
said Lin.
"Quick! We have to catch him!"

The robber ran into the park.

Lin ran after him.
"Lin, stop!" shouted Ed.
"Lin! Ed!" shouted Dad.

Lin chased the robber along a path, across a bridge, and into the zoo!

SPLASH!

he fell into their pool!

Lin caught the bag.
"Got it!" she called.

"CUT!" shouted a man
in a green t-shirt.

"Hey, kid, you were fantastic!" said the man. "We have got our ending."

“What are you talking about?” said Lin.
“What ending?
Is the robber going to jail?”

"No!" said the man.
"We are making a film.
The lady and the robber are actors."

“So they are all actors?” asked Lin.
“Yes,” said the man,
“and you have helped us to finish the film!”

We are film stars!
How cool is that?